# When Sarah Laughed

ISBN 979-8-89112-443-1 (Paperback)
ISBN 979-8-89112-444-8 (Digital)



Covenant Books
11661 Hwy 707
Murrells Inlet, SC 29576
www.covenantbooks.com

# When Sarah Laughed

## A Story of God's Faithfulness

### Genesis 18:1–15; Genesis 21:1–7

Jeanne Dicke

Sarah lived in a tent in the desert with her husband, Abraham. Sarah and Abraham loved God very much. Sarah and Abraham were both old. They did not have any children. This made Sarah sad.

Sarah remembered a promise God made to Abraham a long time ago. It was when God said, "Abraham, I will make you the father of a great nation. You will have as many people in your family as there are stars in the sky."

When Sarah looked up at the stars at night, she wondered, *Abraham and I are so old. How will God keep this promise?* Sarah loved God. She knew God never lied, but how would He keep His promise?

One day when Sarah was in the tent, and Abraham was sitting by the door, three men came to see them. Abraham invited the men to stop and rest.

Then he hurried to get them some food. "Quick, Sarah," he said. "Bake some bread. We have visitors." He told his servants, "Here. Cook this meat. We have visitors."

Then he sat down to talk with the visitors. As they were eating, the men asked Abraham, "Where is your wife, Sarah?" Abraham said, "She is in the tent."

"This time next year," said one of the men, "Sarah will have a son." Sarah heard what the man said.

TEE HEE~

She laughed to herself because she did not believe what he said. *How can I have a baby?* she thought. *I am too old.*

Then the man said to Abraham, "Why did Sarah laugh? Nothing is too hard for God. When I come back in a year, Sarah will have a son."

17

Sarah was afraid. She said, "I didn't laugh."
But the man said, "Yes, you did."

Later, Sarah had a baby boy just like the visitor said she would. Abraham and Sarah were happy. They called their son Isaac, which means "laughter." This time when Sarah laughed, it was because she was happy. She said, "God has brought me laughter. Everyone who hears about this will laugh with me."

God kept His promise and gave Abraham and Sarah a son even though they were both old. God forgave Sarah for not believing that He would keep His promise.

When Isaac grew up, he had two sons. Then his sons had children and their children had children and so on, and so on. Before long, just like God promised, Abraham's family had as many people as there are stars in the sky. God kept His promise to Abraham. Abraham became the father of a great nation.

Many years later a baby boy, who was part of Abraham's family, was born in a stable in Bethlehem. His name was Jesus. Jesus is God's only Son. God sent Jesus to save us from our sins.

God kept His promise to Abraham! God always keeps His promises!

# About the Author

Jeanne Dicke is a retired church worker with experience teaching the Christian faith to individuals with intellectual/developmental disabilities. A first-time author, she has always enjoyed writing for the enjoyment of her family and friends. This book was inspired by a question from her niece, now a mother herself, who wanted to know, "How come nobody writes books about Sarah?"